Artwork © Shutterstock 2024 e14eak90; Blueastro; VectorBoyZ; sasimoto; Kudryashka; Andrii Rymarenko; judyjump; neoncat; PxB; GOLDMAN99; Only _up; Colorfuel Studio; Lusya Lukina; Iliveinoctober

Published by Sequoia Kids Media,
an imprint of Sequoia Publishing & Media, LLC

Sequoia Publishing & Media, LLC,
a division of Phoenix International Publications, Inc.

8501 West Higgins Road, Chicago, Illinois 60631
34 Seymour Street, London W1H 7JE
Heimhuder Straße 81, 20148 Hamburg

CustomerService@PhoenixInternational.com

www.PhoenixInternational.com

Library of Congress Control Number: 2024941889

ISBN: 979-8-7654-0998-5

A-Z Fruits, Veggies, and Me!

Written by Kathleen Hanrahan

An imprint of PHOENIX International Publications, Inc.

Grown from the ground or picked from a tree, fruits and veggies are important parts of a healthy me! These nutritious foods keep Earth healthy, too. There are so many different kinds to enjoy. Just what makes these foods so good?

Fun Fact: Fruits and vegetables are grown on farms or in gardens. Try to get them from places near your home, like a farmers' market or your own garden! The produce will spend less time traveling to your table, which means more nutrients for you and less carbon dioxide for the planet!

I eat apples for fiber, which helps my heart.

B is for **Banana**.

I eat bananas for potassium, which helps my muscles move right.

Fun Fact: An apple a day may keep the doctor away, but don't overdo it! Too many apples, and too much fiber, can cause an upset stomach.

C is for **Carrot**.

I eat carrots for vitamins that help keep my eyes healthy.

D is for **Date**.

I eat dates to help with digestion so my tummy feels good.

Fun Fact: C is also for compost! Composting recycles uneaten fruits and vegetables into nutrient-rich fertilizer. This fertilizer can be used to help grow new produce. Composting can be done at home or through community programs.

E is for **Edamame**.

I eat edamame for protein, which helps my body grow strong.

F is for **Fig**.

I eat figs for a sweet treat that is good for my gut.

Fun Fact: A fig is a fruit, and edamame is a vegetable. One way to tell the difference is the flavor. Fruits are usually sweet or sour, while vegetables are mild and savory.

G is for **Garlic**.

H is for **Horseradish**.

I eat garlic and horseradish to boost my immunity and help protect me from viruses.

Fun Fact: More foods are vegetables than you may think! A vegetable is any part of certain plants, called herbaceous plants, that you can eat. This can include the roots, leaves, stems, and bulbs.

I eat iceberg lettuce in a salad on a hot day to help me hydrate and cool down.

I is for **Iceberg Lettuce**.

J is for **Jackfruit**.

I eat jackfruit to replace meat sometimes, which helps the environment.

Fun Fact: Eating more meat means raising more farm animals, which means smelling more farts! The farts from these animals contain methane, which is a harmful greenhouse gas. Eating more produce can clear the air in more ways than one!

I eat kale for calcium, which helps keep my bones strong.

I use lemon juice on salads with dark leafy greens to help my body absorb iron.

Fun Fact: Kale is known as a superfood. This means it is packed with things like vitamins and antioxidants, which makes it super nutritious. But foods can only really be super when they're part of a super balanced plate!

I eat mangoes for nutrients that help make my skin glow and my hair shiny.

I eat the sea vegetable nori for iodine, which helps my thyroid control my body's most important functions.

Fun Fact: Fruits and vegetables make up half of a balanced plate. The other half should be filled with grains and protein. Whole grains like rice and quinoa and proteins like chicken and tofu make great options to pair with fruits and veggies.

I eat oranges for vitamin C, which helps my body heal when it is hurt.

I eat potatoes for carbohydrates, which give me energy to learn and play.

Fun Fact: Potatoes were the first vegetables to be grown in space! The first vegetable to be both grown and eaten in space was romaine lettuce. Growing food in space can help astronauts eat fresher and healthier!

Q is for **Quince**.

I eat cooked quince as a tasty topping on oatmeal or yogurt.

R is for **Raspberry**.

I eat raspberries for antioxidants that help protect me against diseases.

Fun Fact: Carbohydrates are an important part of a healthy diet. The best carbohydrates are called whole carbohydrates, and they come from foods like fruits, vegetables, and whole grains.

I use spinach to make salad, where I can bring all my favorite fruits and vegetables into one bowl for a nutritious and delicious meal.

Fun Fact: Combining certain foods doesn't just make things tastier—it can also make the dish healthier! Pairing certain salad ingredients with certain dressings, like lemon juice or olive oil, helps your body better absorb the nutrients from the ingredients.

I eat tomatoes as a tasty summer treat from my local farmers' market.

U
is for
Ube.

I eat ube in both sweet and savory ways to help keep my cells healthy.

Fun Fact: Different fruits and vegetables finish growing during different seasons. Eating seasonal produce is healthier for both people and the planet!

V is for **Vidalia Onion.**

I eat Vidalia onions raw to keep my immune system strong while avoiding that strong onion taste!

Fun Fact: V is also for vitamins! These nutrients are necessary for bodies to grow and be healthy. There are 13 essential vitamins, but our bodies can only make two. The rest come from what we eat!

W is for **Watermelon**.

I eat watermelon on a hot summer day to stay hydrated.

I eat *Ximenia* fruit pickled, which gives my body good bacteria to keep my belly balanced.

X is for **Ximenia**.

Fun Fact: Pickled foods are foods that are soaked in vinegar, salt, and other spices. This process makes good bacteria called probiotics.

Y is for **Yuca**.

I eat yuca ground up as a flour that can replace wheat flour in recipes.

Z is for **Zucchini**.

I eat zucchini with its green skin on, which is packed with vitamins and nutrients.

Fun Fact: Flour is used in many recipes. It is usually made from wheat, but can be made from other things like almonds, yuca, or quinoa. Flour made from these more nutritious alternatives can help make the whole dish more nutritious!

They're sweet! They're savory! They're fresh! They're cooked! There are so many kinds of fruits and vegetables and even more ways to eat them. My body, and my planet, thanks me every time they're on my plate.